Dear Alison
Happy Christmas
Best

Rhymes from an
Ancient
A M ariner

By

Norman H. McConochie

APPIN PRESS, UK

First Published 2012 by Appin Press, an imprint of Countyvise Ltd
14 Appin Road, Birkenhead, CH41 9HH

Copyright © 2012 Norman H. McConochie

The right of Norman H. McConochie to be identified as the author of this work has been asserted by him in accordance with the Copyright, Design and Patents Act 1988.

British Library Cataloguing in Publication Data.
A catalogue record for this book is available from the British Library.

ISBN 978 1 906205 87 4

This book is dedicated to the memory of my father
H.A. McConochie, the author of these poems.
Born September 1904, died July 1981.

– CONTENTS –

1. Acknowledgments	1
2. Introduction	3
3. Early Years	5
4. Young Mac	13
5. Marriage and the Sea	19
6. The Good Years	27
7. Family Life Begins	33
8. The Anchor is Swallowed Pro Tem	37
9. Read My Lips	41
10. The Family is Complete	45
11. The War Begins	49
12. A Bird in the Hand	55
13. Kids don't do Stress	59
14. Back to Sea Again	63
15. Englishmen Abroad	71
16. Spiritual Insight	77
17. Twilight to Darkness	81
18. Suffer the Little Children	85
19. Requiem	91

– ACKNOWLEDGEMENTS –

Initially, being unsure how best to proceed with this book, I sought advice and found it from a long standing friend and former shipmate, Len Holder, Master Mariner and academic, himself a prolific writer. I would like to thank him and the publishers he put me in touch with, Countyvise Ltd, who offered so much help.

My thanks also to my wife Bett, and daughters Diane and Jayne who gave much needed practical support and advice, and to my sisters Olive, Jean and Eileen for their contributions and family photographs.

The pictures of SS Inventor and SS Alca were copied from The Gallery of Ship Pictures on the Internet and cannot be separately acknowledged as the owner of the Gallery has no record of the individual donors. I therefore trust that since the proceeds of any sales will go to two charities, any possible infringement of copyright will be overlooked.

– INTRODUCTION –

My father, Herbert Arthur McConochie, ex-seagoing marine engineer and amateur poet, died in 1981 leaving me, amongst other things, his poetry. I followed in his footsteps inasmuch as I also served at sea as an engineer officer, but did not have the wit nor the imagination to write poetry. I wish I had spent more time with him reading the poetry and understanding what inspired him to write it, and I feel ashamed that it has taken me so long to publish some of it for the enjoyment of others. His time at sea was much more varied than mine, having served in a myriad of shipping companies, including T&J Harrisons, Yeoward Brothers, Palm Line, Stanhope Steamship Co., South African Marine and ships run under the control of The Ministry of War Transport. There were a few others, which was perhaps indicative of his restless nature, but it must have given him experience of a wider profile of life and the world than I got in just one company.

There were 85 poems in the collection I received when he died, and I have selected less than half for this publication. If it is successful, a second book may be possible at a later date.

My intention in producing this book is first and foremost to get some recognition of his work, and then to donate any proceeds of the sale to charity, which would no doubt please him greatly if he were here now, as he had a very generous nature.

I hope you enjoy his work.

Norman H. McConochie
January 2012

– EARLY YEARS –

Herbert Arthur McConochie was born 17th September 1904, of working class parents and lived in Wallasey, in a terraced house typical of the time. It had a scullery, living room and parlour downstairs, whilst upstairs were three bedrooms and a bathroom. He had three brothers and one sister, but sadly Jessie his sister, died when quite young, and David the eldest went down with his ship, HMS Black Prince, at the Battle of Jutland in 1916. I am convinced that these two events left a lasting effect on him, which showed up in later life through some of his poetry.

His father was a printer in Liverpool, which was one of the better paid trades at the time, but his mother was in continual bad health which required him to spend a great deal of time away from school, looking after her and running the household. However, despite this disadvantage, he passed the scholarship examination (now called the 'Eleven Plus') to the Wallasey Higher Elementary School, and notwithstanding further long absences from school, his exemplary school reports indicated his excellent grasp of English and the written word, although the main focus of the school's teaching was towards technical subjects.

WALLASEY EDUCATION COMMITTEE.

HIGHER ELEMENTARY SCHOOL

VAUGHAN ROAD, NEW BRIGHTON.

CERTIFIED REPORTS

ON STUDENT'S WORK DURING A

Three YEARS COURSE.

Student's Name   Herbert Maconochie

Date of Birth   September 17th 1904

" " Entrance to the School   August 21st 1917

" " Leaving   July 9th 1920

Previous School from which

entrance Examination was

passed   Manor Rd Council

Youth

What can compare with youth's unsullied view
Of life, and all the splendid things to do;
Such great ideals, such plans of vast intent,
Such eager footsteps ever starwards bent.

And with the dawn the waking sun smiles on
New hopes, new faiths, new trust in every one.
No time to doubt or fear that aught is wrong,
No time to see life's way is hard and long.

Life's far too brief for all the schemes on hand,
Till enters one unasked, that is not planned,
And dwarfs all other things in size, till they
Dwindle to nothingness and pass away.

For with the first sweet pangs of love, no room
Is left for aught but love, and on fate's loom
Another dual pattern springs to view –
Once more the old, old story's told anew.

Yesterday

I wish today was yesterday
And I was born anew;
What different things I'd think and say,
Such different things I'd do.

No harsh word would I speak my love,
No cruel look to bestow;
My thoughts would wing their way above,
Forsake what lies below.

My tawdry pride I'd gladly shed,
And don more humble garb;
I'd try to follow him who bled
From nail and sword and barb.

Today is morrow's yesterday,
I still can mend my way;
Yet when the morrow comes I'll say
'I wish 'twas yesterday'.

LEAVING CERTIFICATE

PRINCIPAL'S REMARKS *On completion of course.*

Herbert R. Machonochie completes his three years' Course with distinction, & the highest credit.

He is a youth of unusual abilities and high attainment. He excels in English Literature, Mathematics, Art Subjects and Geography — a thoroughly good all round lad, — untiring in effort.

By the unanimous vote of the Staff he was elected a "Prefect" of the School — the highest honour the School confers.

It is almost Superfluous to add that his general Character, Conduct, and influence are all that Could be desired. He leaves with our best wishes for his future.

SIGNED _____ W. C. Q. Jones. _____ PRINCIPAL.

ON BEHALF OF EDUCATION COMMITTEE,

_____ John Crawshaw _____ CHAIRMAN.

_____ T. Samuel _____ SECRETARY.

DATE 9th July 1920.

While Watching a Storm

No more the sky its smiling aspect wears,
Its once calm brow seems lined with myriad cares.
Huge sullen looking clouds draw ever near,
The very earth's imbued with breathless fear.

Now all the air a fearful stillness holds,
As awesome as the pall, the bier enfolds;
Save when the wind comes moaning through the trees,
Like tortured souls that know no moments ease.

Heav'ns mighty guns begin their distant note;
The lightning's lurid glare is less remote.
The sky's dark face is marred with ominous frown,
Huge ice-cold shards of rain come hissing down.

Then with a crash the storm lets loose its powers,
The thunder roars, the lightning brighter glow'rs;
The once stout oak lies low in grief and pain;
Flung down to earth, no more to proudly reign.

Upon the sea, its masts all split and riven,
Its sails all torn, the helpless barque is driven.
As some spent stag pursued by countless hounds,
From crest to crest, from trough to trough it bounds.

God's feathered friends, the little birds who cheep
And twitter 'till the sun has gone to sleep,
Are gone, some dead, some driven far to hide;
Far flung the mother from her fledgling's side.

The crofter in his cottage, stark and bare,
Springs up in fear at each unearthly glare,
And sees the ruthless ruin of his toil;
Destruction of his crops, a season's moil.

Why does the God of man this thing allow?
Why crucify the toiler at the plough?
Why let his earthly choir, his warblers gay?
In one short hour be crushed, and flung away?

Evening Star

As slowly dies the sun's last beams
So glimmers forth the evening star;
In solemn state it reigns afar,
Mute herald of approaching dreams.

'Tis but the first of that vast host
of lesser stars; soon will they spread
Their jewelled network overhead;
Sweet charms against the night borne ghost.

Oh Venus you possess the power
To raise the soul to lofty state,
Where fool and mockers cease to prate;
And you supreme for one short hour.

When in the stillness of the night
'Tis vain to woo elusive sleep,
And phantom shapes begin to creep,
Your satellites allay such fright.

Their slender hands reach from above
To soothe the hot and frightened brow,
They whisper 'fear no more enow,
Our mistress sends to you her love'.

You bid your multitude of star
Keep vigil 'till the coming dawn,
When flaming sun puts night to scorn,
And prisons him with golden bars.

– YOUNG MAC –

Having left school at the age of 16, Dad was apprenticed to a firm of Engineers and Ironfounders which manufactured cranes, ship winches and windlasses. He served the statutory 5 years of apprenticeship, during which he attended night school studying technical subjects. On completion of both, he decided to try his hand at seafaring, and accordingly applied to join the well known Liverpool shipping company, T&J Harrison. At some time before first going to sea, he met my mother, Elsie, at a dance, and it seems they both took an immediate liking to each other.

14

This Indenture, made the 13th day of April in the year of Our Lord, One Thousand Nine Hundred and Twenty One

BETWEEN John H. Wilson & Co., Limited, of No. 250, Dock Road, Seacombe, Engineers and Ironfounders, of the one part, and

(Name) *Herbert Arthur Maconochie*

(Address) *45 Greenwood Lane*

Egremont Cheshire

(Age and Date of Birth) *16 Years. 17th September 1904*

with the consent and approval of his *Father*

(Name) *David Maconochie* of the other part

WITNESSETH, that the said *Herbert Arthur Maconochie* doth by these presents, put, place and bind himself a covenant Servant or Apprentice to the said John H. Wilson & Co., Limited, for the time hereinafter mentioned and to be fully completed and ended. AND the said

Herbert Arthur Maconochie doth

covenant, promise and agree to, and with the said John H. Wilson & Co., Limited, that he the said Apprentice shall and will faithfully serve the Company, their secrets keep, their Lawful Commands gladly obey and do; hurt to the Company he shall not do, or suffer to be done by others, when it is in his power to prevent the same; the Company's goods he shall not waste, or embezzle, the same give or lend without leave; shall not absent himself from the Company's service, nor do any other Act, Matter or Thing whatsoever, to the prejudice of the Company, but in all things shall demean and behave himself towards the Company, and all he, as a faithful apprentice ought to do. And the said John H. Wilson & Co., Limited, IN CONSIDERATION hereof,

doth hereby for themselves, their Executors, Administrators and Assigns, covenant, promise and agree to teach, inform and instruct, or cause and procure to be taught, informed and instructed, the said Apprentice, by the best Ways and Means they can in the

Trade of an Engine Fitter

This is to certify that Herbert Arthur Maconochie has duly served his apprenticeship in accordance with the terms of this Indenture

JOHN H. WILSON & CO. LIMITED

Director

THE SCHEDULE REFERRED TO.

SCALE OF WAGES.

1st year at the rate		4/– for every 53 hours worked.		
2nd	do.	5/–	do.	do.
3rd	do.	6/–	do.	do.
4th	do.	8/–	do.	do.
5th	do.	10/–	do.	do.
6th	do.	/–	do.	do.

Recommended by...

On With the Dance

On with the dance, the laughter, and the flirting,
Cast out your woe, your sorry visaged care;
Bind up your wound, make pain cease all its hurting,
Here's help at hand, a hundred maidens fair.

Why spend your life in sorrow and repining?
Mourning that love departed past recall;
Time heals all wounds and gives silver lining
To sorrows clouds, that wrap you like a pall

'Better to have loved and lost' so say the Sages,
'Than ne're have felt love's poignant pangs at all'
Such words of wisdom last throughout the ages,
Come, come my friend and hie you to the ball.

Let music's charm steal o'er you like an incense,
Filling your heart with rapture unalloyed;
Let starry eyes chase vain regrets a league hence,
Let your dull tongue be busily employed.

Heed not the one who loved a while and left thee,
Left you to brood, and view all maids askance;
Spurn her from your thoughts and from your fancy,
Take you some lass, and lead her to the dance.

Play fiddler, play, play you some lightsome measure,
Make you your bow pick out the magic note.
Blow flautist blow, make life to all a pleasure,
Let sweet your trill be trouble's antidote.

If

If I could see you dearest woman,
See you for a short sweet while;
Deep in your eyes I'd gaze dear,
Eyes so candid, without guile.

If I could hear you dearest woman,
Hear your voice so soft and low;
Hear you utter words so tender,
'Dearest man I love you so'.

If I could touch you dearest woman,
Hold you firmly to my breast;
All these things would be my heaven
And my soul's eternal rest.

Do You Remember

Do you remember the night dear?
'Neath the stars and the vapouring clouds;
When Love drifted by on a moonbeam,
And we followed, away from the crowds.

The silence divine was unbroken,
Except for a murmuring sea;
Love looked on and smiled from his chariot,
Then he beckoned to you and to me.

And always when I see the moon dear
Will I think of the night when we rode
Hand in hand on a moonbeam to heaven,
And the stars in your hair winked and glowed.

– MARRIAGE AND THE SEA –

He joined the SS Inventor as 5th Engineer in January 1926 and sailed on her initially for a 4 month voyage. The ship was built for the East African Trade and was launched in 1910, survived the First World War, and was scrapped in 1932.

Herbert & Elsie married in 1927, and set up home in Wallasey. Dad remained with T&J Harrison until 1929, when looking ahead to raising a family, he considered shorter voyages would be more considerate for his 'Dear Lady'.

SS Inventor 1926

Dear Lady

Dear Lady of the shining hair
And eyes that shame the sapphires rare,
Whose cheeks outvie the fairest rose,
Whose skin more smooth than satin shows;
Whose voice in thrilling cadence flows
To charm me as the pipes of Pan
Enchanted tree and rock and man

Methinks that once some angel shape
Perchance found Heaven's gates agape,
And in a mood of wantonness,
And wearied of the sweet duress
In realms that know not strife or stress,
Descended to this earth below,
Where love and hate alternate grow

The heavenly wrath at this rash deed
Was such that God himself decreed,
This soul divine must evermore
Keep earthly bounds and nevermore
Leave Man's confines and upward soar.
Dear Lady this is my surmise,
You came from heaven in mortal guise.

To a Certain Nightdress

O pale pink garment of the night,
So carefully put away;
What hidden charms you hold for me?
Perhaps I'll know some day;
And in the knowing who can tell
To what heights love will rise,
To realms where Venus holds the key
Of golden paradise

The night my love, in you is clad,
That night I hope I'm there;
To feast my eyes on your delight,
To feel my passions flare.
To sense beneath your filmy folds
The source of my great joy;
To glimpse the form that might have caused
Another 'Siege of Troy'.

The time my trembling fingers touched
Your sheer exquisiteness,
The blood leapt madly in my veins,
I would have died for less.
The fierce wild throbbing of my pulse
Was more than I could stand
I closed my eyes, sharp drew my breath,
Let fall the fal'tring hand.

O pale pink vesture of the night
I think some magic pow'rs
Wove into you love's essence rare
To thrill the slumberous hours.
Seduction marks your every strand,
Each thread breathes of desire;
O article of priceless worth,
Voluptuous Night Attire.

HARRISON LINE.

Sept 6th 1926

S.S. "*Inventor*"

To _____

Port of *Manchester*

This is to certify that H. A. Maconochie served on board of the above steamer as 5th Engineer on regular watch from January 2. 26 to May 19th. 26. During that time he was always attentive to his various duties & Strictly Sober.

R. Kinloch
Master

James Simpson
Chief Engineer.

5	CERTIFICATE				6	OF DISCHARGE		6	

Or Certified Extract from List and copy of Report of Character

of Crew and Official Log Book, if desired by the Seaman

No.	*Name of ship and official number, and tonnage.†	Date and place of		*Rating.	Description of voyage.	Report of Character		Signature of (1) Master and of (2) other and official stamp.
		Engagement.*	Discharge.			For ability	For conduct	
1	Intombi 3127	2/1/26 Liverpool	5/5/26 Liverpool	Chief Engineer	Coast Africa	VERY 169 GOOD	VERY 169 GOOD	(1) R. Kirkal (2) 27 MAY 1926 BIRKENHEAD
2	"INTOMBI" S/S. LIVERPOOL – O.N. 131443. – N.T. 2,505. – N.H. & 577.		13.11.26 Liverpool		S. Coast African ports	VERY B37 GOOD	VERY B37 GOOD	(1) E.S. LIVERPOOL (2) NOV 1926
3	S.S. DIRECTOR 147363 Liverpool	22.12.26 Liverpool	7.09.4.27 Liverpool Coast		ports	VERY 194 GOOD	VERY 194 GOOD	(1) LIVERPOOL (2)
4	"Director 147363 Liverpool 3128	11.8.27 Liverpool	30-11-127 Liverpool	Coast	Continental Ports	VERY B11 GOOD	VERY B11 GOOD	(1) LIVERPOOL (2)
5	S.S. ORATOR LIVERPOOL OFF. N. 123007 NET. N. 2945 GR. 4622 N.H. 382	9.2.28 Liverpool	14/4/28 Liverpool	2nd Engr	S. Africa	VERY 197 GOOD	VERY 197 GOOD	(1) G.R. LIVERPOOL (2) 9 JUN 1928 LIVERPOOL
6	do	12/7/28 Liverpool	2/9/28 Liverpool	3rd Eng	ports	VERY 250 GOOD	VERY 250 GOOD	(1) LIVERPOOL (2) 1928

*A" These columns are to be filled in at time of engagement.

† In Eighteen Books must show Horse Power.

R.1663

A Sailor's Plea

Meet me 'neath the moon sweetheart,
Meet me 'neath the star strewn sky;
Meet me very soon sweetheart,
Meet me quick, ere life goes by

Kiss me through the rain sweetheart,
Kiss me through the clouds of tears;
Kiss me yet again sweetheart,
Kiss away the loveless years

Hold me in your arms sweetheart
Hold me 'till the break of day;
Hold me by your charms sweetheart,
Hold me when I'm far away

Morning Watch

The mighty vault of heav'n, its sable face
Bedecked with myriad stars in fairy trace,
Slow moves about the ship's dim outlined sails;
Eight bells ring out, the eastern sky slow pales

Now all is quiet save for the gentle hiss
Of waters gliding by in gurgling bliss;
With now and then the riggings lazy creak,
While whispering winds converse as lovers speak

The vessel slowly heels, it's ruby light
Would seem to set the stygian sea alight;
The murmuring breeze adopts a stronger note,
And night becomes increasingly remote.

The gently swelling sails now proudly show
The pure exquisite lights that swiftly flow
From out the distant sky, where magic brush
Bestows the wak'ning day with rosy blush.

This perfect hour of man, this scene divine,
When soul and sea and sky so close entwine,
And flesh and spirit have no further need
Of lusts, or wants , or any mortal creed.

When time stands still, and to the straining ear
A mermaid's song comes, thrilling, low and clear;
And all the heart cries out with muted voice,
'If there is heaven make this O God, my choice'.

The crimson orb climbs swiftly into sight,
And puts both night and thoughts to hasty flight;
And past recall this moment, so complete
That even Death must recognise defeat.

Grey Eyes

Grey eyes, I humbly bow me to your loveliness,
A loveliness that springs from depths within;
Cool depths that bear no single trace of ugliness,
But gently stir when tender thoughts begin
To peep from out your mind's exquisite portals,
As timid as the fledgling when it tries
Its wings to spread, or as the infant mortals
Attempt unaided steps in sweet surprise.
The beauty of your glance defies my powers
When I assay to capture it in muse;
Your colour is not found 'mongst rarest flowers;
Your light my soul does wondrously suffuse.

– THE GOOD YEARS –

At the beginning of 1930, he joined Yeoward Brothers, a Liverpool based company specialising in fruit imports from The Canary Islands. Over a period of 6 years he sailed on both of their passenger cargo ships, SS Aguila and SS Alca. The voyages were short, 3 weeks followed by a week in Liverpool, which suited him and my mother, and they began thinking about raising a family.

Despite having obtained his superior certificate qualifying as Chief Engineer, the Great Depression had resulted in so many job losses that he was obliged to sail as 3rd Engineer officer. Notwithstanding this, I think he enjoyed his time on these small passenger ships, as he often reminisced about them and the interesting ports of call, such as Santa Cruz in Tenerife.

SS Alca

Whilst Overlooking Santa Cruz

Slowly the soft empurpled shadows deepened,
And kindly starts began their winking gleam;
Wistfully I mused in sweetest silence,
Wishing that I thus could always dream

Like some Olympian God in lofty splendour
I sat, and gazed at Santa Cruz below,
And listened to the sounds that echoed faintly,
Where twinkling lights began their nightly glow.

How my thoughts came crowding, swift and eager,
But greatest of them all, and crystal clear;
That cut a swathe of light through darker fancies,
Thrice precious thought, to have you always near.

The calm and soothing feeling of your nearness
Enveloped me as the mantle of the night;
Dropped gently o'er the town spread out beneath me,
And put more troubled thoughts to hasty flight.

That peace which passeth human understanding
Deep filled my soul, and oh I was so thrilled
To sit and dream, and dream of you forever;
My cup of joy so full it near o'erspilled.

But swift as flies the mother to her fledglings
I came to earth and sadly realised,
My golden hour was over, my sweet dreams ended;
'Twas not for me the love that I most prized.

Now hid the distant toen in velvet blackness,
I shivered with the coming chill night air;
And shivered yet again, for ere the sun rose,
I would be gone, be gone in deep despair.

To a Cruise

I met you on the Ocean's heaving breast,
I stopped, I looked, I loved, that day's thrice blessed;
Life came anew to me, I shed my past,
My heart that once winged free was netted fast.

When first I saw your face, and form divine,
A voice within me murmured 'Make her thine,
Come, press thy suit, plead ardently they cause,
Brook no delay, 'tis only fools that pause'.

Though outward I was calm of face, and voice,
Yet inwardly I feared some other choice
Perhaps was yours, your troth already pled;
Oh, awful thought, it turned my heart to lead.

Sweet thrilling hour when first your lips I pressed,
More thrilling still when I your form caressed;
When in such shy surrender you gave me
A maid's most sacred gift, virginity.

If I could only keep you by my side,
What would I care for wealth, or fame, or pride?
What mean these things to me? If I possessed
The greatest gift of all, love's treasure chest.

CERTIFICATE OF COMPETENCY

AS

FIRST CLASS
ENGINEER No. 70679

OF A STEAMSHIP

To *Herbert Arthur M. Conochie*

WHEREAS it has been reported to us that you have been found duly qualified to fulfil the duties of First Class Engineer of a Steamship in the Merchant Service, we do hereby, in pursuance of the Merchant Shipping Acts, grant you this Certificate of Competency.

BY ORDER OF THE BOARD OF TRADE, this 16th day of December, 1930.

Counter-signed

Registrar General

One of the Assistant Secretaries to the Board of Trade

REGISTERED AT THE OFFICE OF THE REGISTRAR GENERAL OF SHIPPING AND SEAMEN

Dad on left with shipmate on SS Alca circa 1932

What is Love?

What is love? Listen, I will tell you;
Love is a thief, that comes with infant guile
And lends us happiness a while,
Then steals it back, not only that
But all our peace of mind;
And leaves us Life's dull way to wind.

What is Love? Listen I will tell you;
Love is a sham, that cloaks our thought and deed
With rosy hue, and fills our need
Of things not wholly carnal;
Then plucks the film from off our eyes,
And leaves us life in sombre guise.

What is Love? Listen I will tell you;
Love is a fool, that leaves the poets breathless
In their attempts to make him deathless
And constant as the snow clad poles;
Looks on and mocks their disarray,
And with a sigh dies every day.

– FAMILY LIFE BEGINS –

It seemed to me that the period 1930 to 1935 was the most satisfying for both my mother and father, as the short voyages allowed a semblance of contented family life to establish itself. Three weeks away to the Canary Islands, and a week back in Liverpool, even if part of that week was spent aboard ship, was a much more civilised arrangement than long voyages to East Africa and India.

Contentment was soon evident by the arrival of my eldest sister Audrey in September 1930, followed by Olive in December 1932.

Audrey and Olive

Baby Shoes

A toe scraped pair of toddler's shoes,
The first my baby wore.
How loud he gurgled with delight
When first he crossed the floor,
And clutched my gown with chubby hands,
His face with wonder filled
At this, his first great venture when
He'd faltered not, nor spilled

When mem'ry bright, undimmed by years,
I hear again the sound
Of pattering feet from room to room,
Those echoes still abound.
Though now he roams the world afar
With firm and manly stride,
With his first shoes to grace my sight
My babe's still by my side.

Childbirth

The mighty of Heaven, whose bounds begin
And end in dark eternity, stretched high and black;
All stars had ceased to be.
A veil of nothingness lay close about its face;
The sands of time were stilled, the glass unturned.
A breathless hush enclosed the Universe.
The pulsing heart of Earth hung on one beat
Of silent agony; the Gods themselves moved not,
But sat in list'ning attitude.
The quiet was soft broken by a sigh
That held a note of low and stifled pain,
And touched the straining ear as lightly as
A powdered wing might touch a silken strand.
It passed but to return with greater strength
Until the arching trackless void was filled
With wildly rushing winds that sobbed and moaned.
Fiercely they roared as if in mortal strife,
Then ended with a loud triumphant shout.
Out of the still that followed rose a cry,
A new born babe's high pitched protesting plaint;
While through the stygian sky there wanly shone
A lonely winking star. Soft fell the dew
As if the spirits wept in pity for
This soul thrust blindly forth into the World
To fill a destiny it knew not of.
The Earth with shudd'ring sigh once more resumed
Its ordained turning throughout timeless space.

YEOWARD LINE LTD

Telephone
BANK 800

Fleet
S.S. 'ALCA'
S.S. 'AVOCETA'
S.S. 'ALONDRA'
S.S. 'AGUILA'
S.S. 'ARDEOLA'

24, James Street,
LIVERPOOL, 2

*Steamers to Portugal, Madeira and
the Canary Islands*

Telegrams
"YEOLINE"
LIVERPOOL

Directors
R.J. YEOWARD
(managing)
R.R. YEOWARD
B.E. YEOWARD
J.P. WARDLE
W.W. WELSH
B.L. AINSWORTH

20th April.1936.

TO WHOM IT MAY CONCERN.

This is to certify that H.A.Mc Conochie served
as 4th Engineer on the s.s."AGUILA" from January 1930
to December 1930.   He was then promoted to 3rd
Engineer of the s.s."ALCA" and served in that capacity
until January 1936.

During the whole of this time the Chief Engineers
under whom he served always reported very favourably on
his conduct and ability.

He left entirely of his own accord.

J.H. Phillips

Superintendent Engineer.

– THE ANCHOR IS
SWALLOWED – PRO TEM –

Dad was an avid reader and I suspect that unknowingly, most of us in the family became similarly interested in books and any other reading material. Audrey, the eldest, was seldom without a book in her hand and consequently, although not academically minded, she was a hive of knowledge and information, upon which the rest of us drew.

I was born in November 1935, and some months after that, Dad was interviewed for a position ashore as Engineer Surveyor, and being successful, left the sea to continue his career on land.

Dad in middle on SS Aguila, circa 1934

Thoughts after Reading a Newspaper

Every hour into the World
Countless souls are rudely hurled;
Never asked if they would lief
Stay unborn than meet with grief.
Simply made to blindly go
To encounter joy or woe.
Some are born 'midst satins rare,
Never know a want or care;
Never short of wealth or food,
How can they but help be good?
'Tis no merit to those folk
To adopt a saintly cloak;
Easy should it be for those
To be good who have no woes.
But the lot of most mankind
Is to feel that life's unkind;
Poverty and lowly birth,
Years of tilling stubborn earth;
Years of toll in factories grim,
Years all dark and drab and dim;
Rest unknown 'till 'neath the sod;
How can they have faith in God?
Yet if one of them should sin
Comes a wealth of righteous din;
Especially from those who own
Places from which joy has flown.
Factories and mines and mills
Giving man his soul's death chills.
Should the wealthy man's wife steal
Most for her but pity feel;
Look so wise and say 'Alack
She's a Kleptomaniac'.

Should the workless wretch's wife,
Weary of the ceaseless strife,
Steal to feed her hungry flock
Then this gives to most a shock.
Those who want not inward think
'Just another case of drink'
'Why pay we so high a tax?'
'To keep those who live so lax'.
Man his fate does not know of
Even though begat from love;
Nor is asked if he should be
Left unborn eternally.
Whether born to joy or woe
Through the World he's made to go.
Every hour from out the World
Countless souls are rudely hurled.
Never given choice or power
To live on another hour.
Child or youth or aged man
They must end as they began;
They must journey without knowing
Whence or whither they are going.
Man conceives the sacred spark,
God creates the soaring lark.
Man, God says, is born in sin,
How then does the lark begin?
Surely he who knows God's word
Should rank higher than the bird
That does nought but sing and fly,
Then like man is made to die.
All this is a mystery
From which mind and reason flee;
Man must say God's Will be done,
Ending just as he begun,
Not to know from whence he comes,
Or when Death inverts its thumbs.

A Sea Shore Reflection

Close by the mighty ocean's edge I stood,
The booming surf with thunder filled my ears;
My soul was awestruck by this timeless flood
That heeded not the passing of the years;
But rolled unceasing on with changing mood,
Now calm and quiet, now boisterous and rude.

From purpling distance heaved the crestless waves,
Sweeping along with calm unhurried gait;
Rank after rank of Neptune's restless slaves,
Surging they came, resistlessly as fate.
Beyond the power of man to comprehend,
Each wave contained a strength to break, or bend.

Then as they neared the limit of their bounds
They snarled their white fanged challenge to the skies;
Their pace increased like eager unleashed hounds
Responding to the huntsman's urging cries.
They curled and broke with one long hissing roar,
Then gently lapped my feet to be no more.

The path of man throughout this earthly life
Seemed symbolised by nature's grand display;
He comes from out of space to peace, or strife,
Expends his force then quickly fades away.
With nothing is he born, with nothing dies;
Nought left but fading echoes of his cries.

– READ MY LIPS –

As for me, my early reading ability was brought down to earth with a bump, when I was exposed as something of a fraud. I had been taught the basics of letters and reading before first going to school, so felt reasonably confident amongst my peer group. The teacher, I believe her name was Miss Hocking, used a particular book for early reading lessons, and for homework, (yes we had homework in our first year at Primary School), we were required to read certain pages, then demonstrate our ability by reading these pages to the teacher. All was going swimmingly until by accident, (or not, I have never been sure), she turned over 2 pages, and I carried on 'reading' the previous page. I had obviously memorised the pages, a significant feat in its own right I thought in later life, but this cut no ice with Miss Hocking. Back to basics it was for me!

Wishing

If I was like a lark, so free,
I'd fly away from misery;
I'd never know of poverty,
If I was like a lark, so free.

If I was like a fish, so cool,
I'd never have to go to school,
I'd never be a hot head fool,
If I was like a fish, so cool.

If I was like an owl, so wise,
I'd never doubt, or e'en surmise
If this was truth, or that was lies,
If I was like an owl, so wise

If I was like a bear, so strong,
I'd never need to do a wrong,
Or ever use a forked tongue,
If I was like a bear, so strong.

If I was like a lamp, so bright,
I'd never think of day, or night,
I'd never wake up in a fright,
If I was like a lamp, so bright.

But I am not a bird, or fish,
Nor lighted wick in oil filled dish;
I simply sit and wish, and wish;
A Bird? A Bear? A Lamp? A Fish?

Dreamboat

Cast off your gossamer ropes dreamboat,
And with them all waking cares;
Bear me to cool carefree slopes dreamboat,
Where I may find Heaven's stairs.

Ever so slowly you glide dreamboat,
Ever so gently you rock;
Old Father Time is defied dreamboat,
Shorn of his scythe, glass, and smock.

Bright sails of hope o'er you swell dreamboat,
Waters of joy kiss your prow;
Dark mists of pain you repel dreamboat,
Sorrow you will not allow.

Take me not back to awake dreamboat,
Take me not back to the morn;
Let me all mankind forsake dreamboat,
Ever on you to be borne.

– THE FAMILY IS COMPLETE –

After I was born, there followed three more girls, Jean, Eileen and Barbara, and in later life I often joked with Dad that it was my Mother who packed him off to sea again, to avoid the round dozen.

Audrey, who took up nursing after leaving school, married & moved away from the rest of the family. She died in 2006. Olive, the next in line, became, perhaps unwittingly, the family Matriarch. I followed in Dad's footsteps & trained as an Engineer Officer in " The  Blue Funnel Line", ending up as "Fleet General Manager" in OCL which became P&OCL. Jean & Eileen also became senior Nursing Officers, & Jean went on to open & run her own Nursing Home for Geriatrics, before selling it on in retirement.

 Barbara, the baby of the family, married & raised a family, then surprised us all by graduating in English & Sociology at Keele University. She began to show some of the literary leanings of Dad, passed down through family genes. Sadly, before very long she was gripped by that terrible illness Alzheimers, which dragged on & dragged her down inexorably, until she passed away in December 2011 as this book was going to press. At her funeral her daughter Samantha, read one of Dad's poems, " Mourn Ye Not."

The Weaver of Spells

I know a place wherein there dwells,
A woodland sprite all dressed in green,
Who sits her down and weaves her spells;
By mortal eyes she lives unseen.

I saw her once when I was young
And firm believed in fairy folk;
When oft I heard their sweet bells rung,
And understood when flowers spoke

One drowsy summer's afternoon,
As I lay dreaming, tho' awake;
I heard a fairy voice a-tune,
It seemed to come from yonder brake.

With breathless hush my steps I bent
Towards this rare and thrilling sound,
And saw midst copse and bracken pent
A woodland sprite upon the ground.

On magic loom her charms she wove
With threads of rose and golden hue,
And through them all a strand of love
That glistened still with heav'nly dew.

And all the time her fingers sped
In unremitting sweet employ,
These were the words to music said,
Sweet words that brought a sweeter joy.

'I ply my loom and weave my spells,
Heigh nonny ho, Heigh nonny ho
I prison gloom in magic cells,
With a heigh nonny, ho nonny, heigh nonny ho'

I take the strands of golden hue,
Heigh nonny ho, heigh nonny ho,
With busy hands I joy construe,
With a heigh nonny, ho nonny, heigh nonny ho'

As merrily the shuttle flew,
And gnomes and elves did more thread bring,
I spake this sprite of spring time hue
'Please tell me of those spells you sing'
She turned, and looked at me and said
'What is it you would like to know?
Why surely, child 'tis time for bed?
Yet I will tell you ere you go'.

'I weave my spells for young and old,
For all those mortals who believe
That there is more in life than gold;
And over riches do not grieve.'

'For those wise people are akin
To elves and sprites and fairy folk,
Who know that joy springs from within
To ease and lighten trouble's yoke.

All through the day I ply my loom,
And fashion me those things of charm;
Bright wefts of light to challenge gloom,
And warps to parry ills and harm.

When night his sable cloak doth place
Around his sun kissed lady fair,
I take my wares and swift of pace
Forsake my green and shady lair.

While mortals sleep and werewolves prowl,
And goblins grin in silent mirth;
Past whirring bat and hooting owl
I speed my way around the earth.

And over all the dreams of those
Who live their life without complain,
I cast my spells of gold and rose
And put to flight all waking pain'

Thus spake that woodland sprite to me,
In tones as clear as tinkling bells.
I see her still in memory,
I still believe me in her spells.

49

– THE WAR BEGINS –

Air Raid Wardens, Dad farthest right

Dad was a softie where animals were concerned. When war broke out we were living in North Harrow, Greater London and then moved to Cheam in Surrey, as the dictates of his job as engineer surveyor required. Despite the demands of his work, and in common with so many other civilian occupations, he was in both the Home Guard and the ARP (Air Raid Patrol) Much to the frustration of my mother, but to the delight of the rest of us, he would frequently arrive home after a busy patrol of night air raids with an orphaned dog left destitute in the streets.

To a Painting

Dear little Scottie dog, faithful and true,
What more could I desire if I had you
To help me on life's way, to make me feel
I had a friendship that no one could steal.

Oft do I gaze at your kind wistful face,
Oft do I wish that my hearth you would grace;
Deeply I envy the one who possessed
Such a great wealth of love, heavn'ly bequest.

All my ambitions to you I'd confide,
Stoutly I'd face the world, you by my side;
Knowing full well that if aught went amiss
You would still cleave to me, never remiss.

And of a night when the day's toil is o'er,
And we had shut out the world with the door;
Shut out the weal and the woe and the strife,
And all the sordidness of daily life.

Filled with content I would sit at my ease,
Smoking my pipe, with your head on my knees;
No need to speak, or to laugh, or to joke;
Just a brief tail wag, a pat, or a stroke.

Thus do I dream as I sit with my pen
Writing and musing, and thinking of when
I shall meet him whose true likeness I hold;
He who possesses a heart of pure gold.

Twighlight

Firelight flickering, sparrows bickering,
Cool grey close of an autumn day;
Mem'ries mingling, dead hopes tingling,
Old tired eyes gaze the eve away

Flames less agile dance, shadows close advance,
Fireborn pictures lose shape and fade;
Eyelids softly close, starlight faintly shows,
Dreams glide by on their night parade.

Daybreak

Softly and slow the pale tipped hands of waking dawn
Gently caressed the dark browed eastern sky;
Distant and clear a cockerel's shrill and strident horn
Wound fleeing night a last defiant cry

Frail wisps of clouds like vapours from a panting steed
Snared and enmeshed Apollo's golden lance.
Down by the marsh a vagrant wind made rush and reed
Curtsey and bow in sleepy headed dance.

Few were the stars that braved the bright hued hosts of day,
Palely they glowed, then feebly flickered out;
Fancy portrayed the Sun God's steeds in proud array
Chafing to put their sable foe to rout.

With true royal air the King of Day his presence showed,
Lowly the gaze beneath his flashing mien;
Crimson and gold his armies by his chariot strode,
Day had arrived in all his glittering sheen.

Patience

There are times when we are tired,
There are times when hope's expired,
There are times when we are sad and sore afraid;
When the soul in deep dejection
With the head bows in subjection,
And we feel that we can never make the grade.

Maybe trouble is a 'Trailmate',
Maybe poverty cries 'Stalemate',
Maybe Death deprives us of our dearest one;
When our prayers seem quite unheeded,
And we feel wc are not needed,
And a shoulder we would have to lean upon.

Think then of the 'Great Provider'
Who e'en makes the lowly spider,
And endows it with a patience past our ken;
Tho' we break its web four score times
Yet as oft to mend it, it climbs,
Let us not outvie the fortitude of men.

Such a gift does God bequeathe us
Like stout armour to ensheathe us,
And protect us with a garb of shining steel;
Yet the will to take and wear it,
Feel its weight, yet grin, and bear it,
Lies with man, and thus to man must man appeal

– A BIRD IN THE HAND –

Later on when we had moved yet again, this time back to Wallasey, I recall going to New Brighton model boat pool with Dad and Olive, it was 1943 and shortly before he returned to sea.. A seagull with oiled wings was in the middle of the pool, unable to fly whilst the local children were using it as target practice. Without hesitation, Dad took off his shoes, rolled up his trousers and waded in and rescued the unlucky bird, and we took it home. Over several days he cleaned the oil from its feathers, and we all took it in turns to feed it. It had the run of a large sunroom, with windows front and back, which we opened each day, but it seemed quite happy to remain with us. It did fly off several times and returned, but finally it went for good. Quite the reverse of what happened to the albatross in 'The Rhyme of the Ancient Mariner'.

Thanksgiving

Swift as the lark in upward trend
Your soul makes joyous flight;
Clear as his notes to heaven ascend,
Your muse to gloom brought light.

For that foul Demon men call Doubt
Had cankered deep my heart;
Your words were charms that cast him out,
Revived my dying art.

How can I thank you, Oh my friend?
Reveal my gratitude?
For on that road that has no end
I tread with strength renewed

Although my muse in humbler mould
Than yours is cast, I pray
That in it will I live when cold,
For ever and a day

Soar ever starwards valiant soul,
Wing fast your way on high;
May words as rich as ermined stole
Enfold you 'till you die.

Why?

God made the stars, the sun, the moon,
To fill the dark and desolate sky;
The fairest flower, the rose in June,
He fashioned and man asked not 'Why?'.

The gentle rain from heaven above
Was sent in answer to man's cry;
Was sent as token of his love,
His love for those who asked not 'Why?'

Mankind did form from brass and steel
Huge creatures that abused the eye;
Grim soulless things that could not feel,
That toiled and moiled and asked not 'Why?'

They did but serve the greedy few,
Who nought but gold could e'er espy,
Who to their wealth would wealth accrue,
Knew mankind's wants, yet asked not 'Why?'

Now when these robots took command
And slave the master did defy,
And workless thousands filled the land,
Man turned to God and asked him 'Why?'

Supplication (2)

Lord God on high
Let me not die
Yet, but one hour grim Death defy;
Just for a while
May beauty's smile
Brighten my way, my last dark mile.

Beauty of face,
Beauty of grace,
Beauty of faith to take doubt's place;
Beauty of thought,
Beauty hand wrought,
Beauty that lives when man is nought.

Ugly my youth,
Ugly forsooth
Were all the years I knew not truth;
Ugly my life
Ugliness rife
Throughout my years of worldy strife.

Lord God on high,
Hear thou my cry,
Grant me thy mercy ere I die;
Answer my prayer,
Lighten my care;
Let beauty's touch relieve despair.

– KIDS DON'T DO STRESS –

Whilst the war years must have been incredibly stressful for adults particularly so for those with young families, for my sisters and I, it was a happy time. We didn't have responsibilities, and didn't appreciate the dangers nor the severe problems facing our country. Mum and Dad kept us fed and clothed, and like many others they rearranged the garden to 'dig for victory' so that we were not short of fresh produce. Christmases were great fun with most of us getting homemade presents which we had helped make in the run up to Christmas Eve. A very long and old red dressing gown and hood was well used every year, with belief on our part initially, followed by connivance for fear of being excluded from the ritual. Father Christmas never let us down.

A Merry Christmas?

'Twas Christmas Eve and through the driving sleet
Sped countless pairs of eager squelching feet;
On joyous festive errands were they bent,
The savings of a year they gladly spent.

The glist'ning street reflected in its face
The gay illuminated shops in which no trace
Of poverty or want could be defined;
They catered for the purse that was well lined.

Bright flashing signs gave forth a brave display;
A hundred thousand lights held night at bay.
On every side were handshakes, greetings, cries;
And wonderings of the morrow's glad surprise.

Close by a shop most lavishly endowed,
Unheeded 'midst the happy jostling crowd,
Two children of the slums stood, hand in hand,
And looked with awe at food and toys so grand.

Said Judy to her brother, Bill aged ten,
'Is this where farver Christmas comes for when
He wants to get a lot more Christmas toys,
To take to uvver little girls and boys'.

'There ain't no farver Christmas', Bill replied,
'Cos when I asked me mum she only cried,
And when I asked me dad he only sed
I wished there was mebbe he'd bring us bread'.

In sodden rags, with features wan and pinched,
And puny forms that at the coldness flinched;
They pressed their faces 'gainst the steaming pane.
Their hearts were filled with wishes, wild and vain.

'Wot would yer like supposing it was true'
Said Judy, teeth a-chatter, lips near blue.
And Bill replied with what was near a sob,
'I'd like me dad to go and find a job'.

Spoke Judy with a very thoughtful look
'I'd like a nice big fire and lots to cook,
Like bacon, taties, tripe and pigs feet too,
And two or three big plates of nice hot stew'.

Poor Bill he could not stand this any more,
And at his sister, 'tho so young, he swore;
And homeward turned his steps, his heart like lead;
No fire, no food, and sacking for his bed.

Now reader, please allow me one more word,
If this, your heart, has not already stirred.
Just spare a trifle, never mind how small,
And make this Christmas Merry, ONE AND ALL.

Suffer Little Children

A pain wracked cripple child made prayer to seek
'The Gentle Healer', keeper of the meek
In spirit and the pure in heart;
And through the solemn stillness of the night
Her lisping speech, if I remember right,
Went thus, and this I heard.
'B'ess mummy and B'ess daddy dear, B'ess nanny and B'ess tim;
'Cos Tim's my doggy, I love him,
And b'ess my dolly too;
P'ease make me well, keep safe this night,
And in the morning when I'se wake, make bright
The sun's kissed face, Amen'.
The Angels smiled to hear such simple faith and trust
In him whose Father into dust
Breathed life everlasting.
Then looking to their Master's radiant face they sighed,
And swiftly winged their way beside
The restless tossing child;
And in her troubled sleep she turned, and smiled to hear
The rustle of Celestial Pinions near
To keep her safe,
But at their Master's bidding they stooped o'er
The body freed from pain, and gently bore
Her soul to realms above.
And clear above the weeping of the crowd I heard
A voice divine repeat the holy word,
'To come unto me'
'Suffer little children to come unto me, for
Of such is the Kingdom of Heaven', nor
Boasts Lucifer one infant soul.

– BACK TO SEA AGAIN –

In late 1943, Dad decided to return to sea, and initially sailed in the Arctic convoys to Russia, on SS Empire Carpenter. The conditions were, by all accounts pretty uncomfortable. After further service under Ministry of War Transport control, he joined The Stanhope Steamship Company, owned by Jack Billmier, a well known and highly respected ship owner, who had made his fortune during the Spanish Civil War of 1937-1939.

By this time Dad was sailing as Chief Engineer.

Unfortunately, in 1947, after 6 consecutive voyages on the SS Stanhill, it was wrecked after running aground off the Ivory Coast, whilst on passage from Lagos to Glasgow. The ship was abandoned, all hands taking to the lifeboats, and luckily they were picked up by another Company ship, SS Stancourt.

Coincidently, many years later, probably around 1985, when I was Fleet General Manager in Overseas Containers Ltd., I discovered that an older colleague had been a deck apprentice on the same unfortunate voyage, and remembered the Chief Engineer well. By that time, my father had long since passed away.

SS Stancleeve 1949

Atlantic Gale

Fierce snarled the waves with bare uplifted fangs,
Cruelly the vessel's side they mauled;
Tearing and grinding with dull soul sickening clangs;
Loud groaned the hull to feel those awful pangs;
By death she lay, close walled.

Shrill screamed the wind as if it was Hell sent,
Weirdly it shrieked and gasped.
Swift rushed it's blasts defiantly death bent;
Weak throbbed her screw, dejectedly and spent.
Roughly her rivets rasped.

Stiff crouched her crew with ashen weary faces,
Stark staring fear they knew.
Of rafts and boats there were no slightest traces,
Clear was she swept from trunk to mainmast braces;
Wildly the storm scud flew.

Then came a wave that brushed the leaden sky,
High o'er the ship it hung;
Mad;y it broke with one long hissing sigh,
Nor was there heard one feeble human cry;
Deep was she coldly flung.

The 'Bay'

With slatting lines and bellied sails
She drove before the freshing breeze,
The waters hissed against her rails
In great unease.

Across the dreaded 'Bay' she flayed
To meet a fate she knew not of;
And every soul aboard her prayed
To God above.

'O Lord keep safe this ship tonight
And guard her from all dangers near;
Grant we soon see the homestead light,
And kinsfolk dear'

The brassy sun slid out of sight,
The wind commenced to moan and shrill;
A ring-ed moon showed wan and white,
Foreboding ill.

The seas began to snarl and roar
Beneath the Storm God's gusty lash,
Against the vessels side they tore
With thund'ring crash.

Sail after sail was quickly furled,
'Till nought was left but gaunt bare masts;
Still higher were the combers hurled,
By mighty blasts.

As some spent stag she faltered on,
While bayed the wind like hounds in cry;
And fainter still the pale moon shone,
With baleful eye.

Soon massing clouds engulfed the moon,
And all around lay black as sin;
The wind struck up a wilder tune,
A hellish din.

Inside the foc'sle dark and dim
Stiff crouched the crew in sodden gear,
Their faces 'neath the lantern's glim
Were blanched with fear.
Deep rolled the thunder's booming note,
The lightning's vivid searing blade
Revealed the stricken barque remote
From help or aid.

A mighty wave with foaming crest
Bore down upon the helpless ship
To snatch her closely to its breast
In cruel grip

An awful tearing rending crash,
A dreadful sobbing shrieking roar,
And by a lurid purple flash
She showed no more.

The homestead lights send out their gleam,
And loving hearts keep watch and pray;
But those they love forever dream
Deep in the 'Bay'

On Being Called in the Morning

Faint stirs the brain at this, the rude awak'ning knock;
Slow it responds with tired reluctant feet.
Vain does it strive to shut those cursed echoes out;
Echoes that sound with dull insistent beat.

Out of the realm of sweet delight and pleasure deep
Drifts back the mind with feeble halting gait;
Loath to depart from slumbers warm and tender clasp;
Loath to return and don the waking state.

Would that the soul could constant sleep, and ever dream,
Never to meet the harsh demands of life;
Never to wake and shiver at the greying dawn
Bringing another day of toil and strife.

From the Diary of a 'Tramp' Chief Engineer

Come, list to my tale of today, not of old;
Of Billie and Bob, two big boilers, and bold.
They hissed and they panted by day and by night;
And when they 'Blew Off' t'was a wonderful sight.

Now Billie and Bob, when this story began,
Were put on a ship named 'Stancleeve', (that's our Stan).
Their job was to steam and make 'Ernie alive,
With 'revs' thirty to forty, and at times seventy five.

Now 'Ernie's' the engine with piston and cranks;
And cylinders and crossheads, and valve gear that clanks.
And gives to 'Our Stan' all the speed he requires;
So in Billie and Bob must be put roaring fires.

These fires boil the water that both boilers need,
The bigger the fires the better the speed.
'Tho Billie and Bob are a grumbling pair,
And often cry 'Chief', 'tis so hot, easy there.

Yet when the 'Old Man' says 'Now Stan, hurry lad',
Then Billie and Bob go on steaming like mad;
And round goes our 'Ernie' with vigour renewed,
Like a hungry man filled up with all kinds of food.

They're all good pals really, if truth but be said;
Though they all of great gales have a bit of a dread.
Which calls to mind once, when out West they were bound,
To a port called St. Johns, in the 'Land' named 'New Found'!

They set off from Tyneside with 'nowt' in the holds,
'Twas winter, and all of them suffered from colds.
Poor 'Stan' had the shivers, oh how his plates shook,
Whilst Billie and Bob had a feverish look.

The weather was stormy, but not very bad,
Though the way 'Ernie' went you'd have thought he was mad.
For first he'd go slow, and then practically stop,
Then suddenly start spinning as fast as a top.

Past Dover the Channel was just like a pond,
And not even 'Stan' could guess what lay beyond
Past Portsmouth they glided, past Southampton too,
And waters once green began now to look blue.

'Glass is falling' says Captain to Chief Engineer,
And he spoke in a whisper so's Stan couldn't hear;
'Ay! It looks rather bad' replied Chief with a frown,
'I'm worried about 'Ernie' I'd better go down'

So down to the engine room Chief slowly trod,
And looked at each nut, and each bolt, and each rod;
And said to our 'Ernie' 'Stop acting like mad'
'Just steady yourself now, there's a good lad'

Now 'Ernie could see by grim look in Chief's face,
'Twas no time for larking, he'd better not race;
So giving a clink and a clank of his parts,
He settled down steady, and stopped fits and starts.

At last all the land had been left far behind,
And size of the waves made 'Stan' troubled in mind;
They slapped him and pushed him and sprayed him all o'er,
While up came the wind with a snort and a roar.

Night deepend, and all was a s black as could be,
One couldn't find sky, and one couldn't find sea;
The waves became bigger as each minute passed,
They clutched tight hold of 'Stan' and held on to him fast.

Now while 'Stan' was rolling, and tossing about,
From out of the engine room came a great shout;
It seemed that the sea water had entered stokehold,
And while 'Billie' was steaming poor 'Bob' was stone cold.

For all 'Bobbie's' fires had gone out with a hiss,
And 'Ernie' had shouted 'I cannot stand this,
I'm stopping, I'm stopping, I've not enough steam,
I think poor old 'Bob' must have busted a seam'.

Down ladders came Chief with a terrible rush,
He spoke sharply to 'Ernie', and near made him blush;
'Pipe down you big softie, what's all this about?
There's nowt wrong with Bob, only fires that's out'

The fires were soon lit and made 'Bob' nice and warm,
Whilst all around 'Stan' raged and blustered the storm.
Said Captain to Chiefie "Wouldst care for a sup?
I think worst is over, see glass going up'.

By morning the storm had abated somewhat,
And 'Billie' and 'Bob' were all steaming and hot;
Our 'Ernie' spun round with a gay carefree air,
And showed not one sign of his last night's despair.

– ENGLISHMEN ABROAD –

By the time I made my first voyage to sea in 1954, Dad was in his final decade of seafaring, and I assumed that our paths would not pass for many years to come. Surprisingly though, outward bound on that first trip to the Far East, I received a radio message from him indicating that we may well pass in the Suez Canal, his ship Northbound and mine Southbound. Sure enough, whilst we were anchored in The Great Bitter Lake, awaiting the Northbound convoy, there he was on the deck of his ship waving something large and white. It turned out it was the fourth Engineer's shirt!

During my relatively short seafaring career of ten years, I had the good fortune to meet up with him three times more, in Japan, Singapore and Hamburg. In Japan, his ship was in drydock undergoing major hull repairs, after having a pretty arduous life carrying a variety of mainly bulk cargoes, and being worked very hard without the necessary and essential maintenance being carried out. Finally, the Classification Society called a halt to further trading until these major repairs were undertaken. I remember he was quite scathing of the way some shipowners operated.

The Money Maker

Only a vessel that passed in the night;
Vague shadow shape with dull winking light.
Rolling along with a lumb'ring gait;
Bound with cargo of rails for the 'Plate'.

'Tuskar' lay flashing and dropping astern;
Cranky old engines kept slowly a-turn.
Wheezing and groaning their note of protest,
Forty years toiling and hardly a rest.

Heaving and pitching for forty long years;
Fog bound in the 'Puget', heat dazed of Algiers.
Often near swamped by an Indian monsoon;
Battered and bruised by a South Sea typhoon.

Then there were times when her mistress, the sea,
Put on a mood of sweet tranquillity.
Leaving the ship to nose perfectly on;
Dreaming her dreams of a glory, long gone.

Proud was the day when she first left the slips,
Regal her air as she passed other ships.
First of her kind she was treated with awe;
None but the finest of cargoes she bore.

Hoary old sea dogs of clipper renown,
Spoke of her runs with a sneer and a frown.
'Give us a ship like the Thermopylae,
Then we will show what a good run should be'

But in the joy of her new strength and pride
She heeded not of the wind, sea, or tide.
Head seas or beam seas, or seas close behind,
Steady her pace and a course clear defined.

Then with the passing of time passed her fame;
No one to laud her, just nearly a name.
One of ten thousand, bereft of all pride.
Harried and driven, and oft sorely tried.

Strange were her cargoes and countless her ports
Desperate her conflicts with Neptune's cohorts;
Squat rusted figure, sans beauty, sans grace.
Dirty and dented, and tardy of pace.

Here's to her passage, a safe one and sound;
Confusion to dangers that ever abound.
A speedy discharge, then cargo for home;
And give her her due when she ceases to roam.

An Echo of the 'Unsworth' Tragedy

Stumbling and stagg'ring with funnel salt encrusted,
Blindly she drove to meet her hastening doom;
Loud groaned her hull, with many a dent, and rusted;
Fierce raged the seas, and gathered fast the gloom.

Crouched on the bridge, their faces grim and weary,
Huddled those men who fought a losing fight.
Ceaselessly they watched with eyes red rimmed and bleary,
Pitting their skill against the ocean's might.

Gone were her masts, and with them gone for ever
Twin magic strands of copper woven wire;
Without these wires their call for help would never
Reach other ships; all hopes must now expire.

Gone too her boats, their pieces strewed the waters,
Crushed like shell beneath some vandal heel;
Clear rose the song of Neptune's siren daughters,
Soon would her crew their chill wet kisses feel.

Lower she sank 'till o'er the deck the waves broke,
Hissing and writhing like some monstrous form.
Thro' the stygian night not e'en the smallest star woke,
Nought left but man to face the awful storm.

Shudd'ring she stopped, hung for one breathless moment,
Poised like a hawk about to make its swoop;
Deep, deep, she plunged, all power to keep afloat spent;
Slid out of sight, from stem to shattered poop.

High o'er the storm the 'Furies' rode the faster;
Sisters of fate, turmoil and despair;
Loud shrilled their glee as sped they to their Master.
News of success they brought Him to His Lair.

A Tramp Ship

In the foc'sle there was silence
As they listened to the vi'lence
Of the worst nor'wester ever known to blow;
Tow'ring waves in wind lashed fury
Were as hangmen, judge, and jury,
Waiting restlessly to deal their deadly blow.

For a time they sat in fear,
Half aware that death was near;
And the night was black as Satan's stinking hell.
By the smoking lamp's dull glimmer,
(No one cared a jot to trim 'er,)
Ev'ry face showed signs that they could hear their knell.

There Antonio Pirelli
Shook and shivered like a jelly,
For already had he died a thousand times;
Said Tom Jones, the old sea lawyer
'By the dirty slut that bore yer,
Yer but paying for yer lousy dago crimes.'

Spoke the bosun Olaf Larson,
Son of a Norwegian parson;
'Dis is vere ve sign off mit out enny pay'
The grim humour of his statement,
Of their fear caused some abatement,
Though they sensed they'd never see the break o day.

All their lives had been lived crudely,
Oft they cursed each other lewdly,
Fought as fierce and wild as any jungle pair;
Yet without these tough old sea dogs,
Who feared only God, and thick fogs,
We would never know our silks and spices rare.

Of her boats there were no traces,
At their best they were disgraces;
Tho' these details shore folk never seem to heed.
She was undermanned, deep laden,
Ev'ry man was an ill paid 'un,
Victims of an owner's soulless grasping greed.

With a lurch and with a shudder
She unshipped her damaged rudder,
Took a sea that swept her bare from stem to stern;
Then a mighty wave approached her,
Caught her helpless, smashed and broached her,
Down she plunged with screw still vainly on the turn.

In the foc'sle there was silence
And they feared no more the vi'lence
Of the worst nor'wester man had ever known;
There Tom Jones from Abergele,
Squarehead bos'un and Pirelli
Were as motionless and cold as lumps of stone.

They had reached the final haven
Of the brave, and of the craven;
Each had been allotted his respective berth;
From the youngest to the oldest,
From the scaredest to the boldest
They had signed from off the Articles of Earth

– SPIRITUAL INSIGHT? –

Writing of any kind, but perhaps poetry more than prose, requires an imaginative mind and some deep thought verging on introspection. I can see this now in Dad through reading his poems, better than I could when he was alive. He didn't attend church much, but retained a strong belief in the Almighty, and at the same time was something of a spiritualist. At one point, according to my sister Olive, he became involved in a ghost hunting group, but I have no further knowledge of its activities, and only know that a couple of his poems seem to reflect either his thoughts or his fear.

I Saw a Ghost

I saw a ghost, a spectre grey and grim,
With grisly leering face and caverns dim
Wherein the eyes were not, and at my side
It stood; this relic of my fallen pride.

False pride, 'twas but a little time ago
It minced and flaunted with its gaudy show
Of haughtiness and proud disdain, which served
To hide that mocking ghoul, all unobserved.

Truth plucked, from off this monstrous piece of sham,
(Which slyly whispered 'As thou art I am')
Its false array, and left this hideous part;
(Which slyly whispers 'As I am thou art')

Fear

What is this 'Thing' I think I feel,
I think I hear and see?
That seems in every dark filled spot
To lurk malevolently.
When night has spread its sable pall,
And vampires grin and glower,
Then comes this 'Thing' to mar my sleep,
To haunt my waking hour

O Gracious God, cast out my fear
Of this 'Thing' worse than death.
Heavens, can I feel upon my cheek
Its rank and fetid breath?
Is that its hand upon my wrist,
That cold and corpse like grip?
Do grave spewed tones sound in my ears?
My footsteps halt and trip

These things seem real, yet are they real?
This 'Thing' is, it is not;
I force my faltering footsteps to
Take me from this cursed spot.
Look, see that nook deep shadow filled,
That place with ghoulish air,
Can you see something blacker still?
Is something hiding there?

I pause, I stop, I turn around,
My footsteps to retrace,
Dear God, what is it I glimpse now?
Was that some demon face?
What was that form that barred my path?
That shape of dev'lish mould?
It is, 'tis not, my way is clear;
Sweet peace my soul enfold.

Fog

How coldly swirls the voiceless fog,
Its clammy shroud enfolding
Tall mast and spar and lifeless sail;
The bowsprits gilded moulding

Its breath subdues, as death subdues
The boldest of the bold;
Its touch lies light on ship and man;
Yet firm its grasp, and cold.

No sound is heard except for when
The strident fog horn blares;
The very yard arms still their squeak,
The stoutest heart despairs.

Vast grotesque shapes half form then fade,
Return, then fade again;
As phantom mutes in ghostly play
Cavort in dim arraign.

That sense of utter helplessness,
That dread of what is not;
Deep fills the heart of every man,
Of such is fear begot.

Then when that spectral veil is rent,
And staring eyes relax;
Deep gratitude fills every heart;
And every heart cries 'Pax'.

Rough voices that were hushed with awe
Regain their brazen note;
The bellied sails and hissing wake
Drive nameless fears remote.

– TWIGHLIGHT TO DARKNESS –

My mother died of a stroke on Easter day 1975, and whilst Dad lived on for a further six years, he had lost his life's partner and life's meaning. He died in July 1981.

A Sailor's Prayer

Hear Thou my simple prayer O God, grant me but one request,
Let not my bones be earth enclosed when I have gone to rest;
For when the time has come to take my last unwaking sleep,
Then would I lie in waters blue, full sixty fathoms deep;
Full sixty fathoms deep O Lord, remote from toil and strife;
Hear Thou this simple sailor's prayer, Creator of all life.

Mourn Ye Not

Now mourn ye not for those who die
In service of the Lord;
For they rejoice midst hosts on high,
And live the Holy Word

No matter how their death was caused,
How long or short their span;
They kept their faith in God nor paused
To doubt his holy plan

And if ye likewise do as they,
Keep faith as they have kept;
Then shall thy sins be washed away
By tears that Christ has wept.

For he hath wept for all mankind,
Atoned for all their sin;
He healed the halt, the lame, the blind,
Made pure the heart within.

So Brethren waste not time in tears,
Come, buckle on your shield,
And sally forth throughout the years
The sword of faith to wield.

A Sailor's Lullaby

Blue restless sea 'neath cloudless glitt'ring sky,
White foaming wake, and gulls awheel on high.
Tall slender masts that stretch their hands to heav'n,
Proud sails like swans in fairy harness driv'n.

Huge tow'ring waves that brush the drab hued sky,
Lee rails awash, and ne'er a garment dry;
Bare wind whip't poles that shrill their plaintive note;
Wide boundless space, could man feel more remote?

Lure of the sea in calm or angry mood
Thrums my heart strings with gentle breath, or rude.
Give me a ship, a sea, a changing sky,
Come winds and sing a sailor's lullaby.

– SUFFER THE LITTLE CHILDREN –

Dad had not written any poetry for many years before his death, his last work being 'The Shrimp in King Neptune's court' which he composed for his grandchildren. It has 26 verses in the first episode which I have included here, leaving the second episode for another time.

The Grandchildren circa 1960/1970, of:

Audrey

Olive

Norman

Jean

Eileen

Barbara

On How the Humble Shrimp Gained a Title and Changed the Colour of his Coat

At good King Neptune's court one day,
A tiny shrimp was heard to say,
'Your Majesty, I humbly beg',
Then stopped, and made a graceful leg

King Neptune seemed to take no heed,
Just stroked his beard of green seaweed,
And sat as if beneath a spell,
Upon his throne of pearly shell.

The poor shrimp wiggled to and fro,
Then made a move as if to go;
Stopped, turned, and looked, and tried to speak,
But only gave a watery squeak.

The Monarch slowly turned his head,
Smiled at the shrimp and softly said,
'What is it you require of me?,
Fear not, I always heed a plea'.

The shrimp coughed once, then tried to find,
The words for what he had in mind;
Bowed several times and then began,
And this is how his story ran.

'We are but humble shrimps O sire,
Not worthy of your kindly ire,
But underneath our coats of grey,
Our hearts are loyal, true and gay'.

For some time past we've heard it said
Your majesty desired to wed,
But though you sought both far and wide,
You failed to find a worthy bride.

The shrimp then stopped as if dismayed,
To see his boldness thus portrayed;
And blushed from head to tip of toes,
And turned from humble grey to rose.

'Proceed' the King said with a smile,
'Fear not, my interest you beguile;
'Tis true of late I've felt alone,
With no fair maid to share my throne'.

The shrimp with courage thus renewed,
And with true loyalty imbued,
Began once more to tell his tale;
Whilst nearby slept an ancient whale.

'The other day there came to me
A cousin from a distant sea;
A rambler who had travelled far
O'er stone and shingle, reef and bar'.

'Among the many tales he told,
Of pearls and coral, icebergs cold;
Was one about a mermaid fair,
Whose grace and beauty none could share'.

'Her tresses were of silv'ry green,
Her tail had blue and golden sheen,
Her suiters woo'd and woo'd in vain,
She glance but once, then ne'er again'.

'She dwells afar in lonely state,
For any King a fitting mate.
Your Majesty, most gracious sire,
I ask permission to retire.'

Now at these words King Neptune's air
Of melancholy and despair,
Began to lift, like morning mist,
That by the sun is softly kissed.

And over all the oceans deep,
And in cool depths where sailors sleep,
A whisper sped of glad refrain;
'Our gracious sire knows joy again'.

With kindly mien the King then spake,
'Sir Shrimp my gloom I now forsake,
I feel as if I'm free from spells;
Pray tell me where this damsel dwells?'.

'O King' replied the shrimp with joy,
(For now a title he'd employ)
'This mermaid dwells in distant climes,
Where every eve the conch bell chimes.'

'With waters blue and waters green,
And sand the purest ever seen,
There does this maid cavort and play,
Not many leagues from Mandalay'.

'So if you seek this treasure rare,
Your finest coach you must prepare;
And send to her in splendid state
Your most entrusted potentate'.

Then spake the King in royal tones,
'Ho dolphins here, come lazybones,
Take my sea coach of coral pink,
Nor tarry ye to preen and prink'.

'But with all speed and no delay,
Begone ye now to Mandalay;
And I shall send in splendid state
My most entrusted potentate.'

And with a truly regal air,
Then King spake to all subjects there,
'Sir Shrimp shall have this honoured post,
Of all my court I trust him most.'

With swelling heart and joyful pride,
Sir Shrimp unto the King replied,
'I thank thee sire, but look, I pray
At this my dingy coat of grey'.

'Fear not my friend' the Monarch said,
'Henceforth this coat of grey you'll shed;
For faithful have you been and true,
Here, take this coat of crimson hue.'

So off Sir Shrimp, in splendid state
Befitting such a potentate,
Sped swiftly o'er the ocean's bed;
And that is how the shrimp turned red.

– REQUIEM –

Looking back now, I can see an aspect of his character which had escaped me as a child, and later on I was too involved in my own career and family life to give much attention to this. I believe he was always searching for something he never quite found, in spite of a busy and fulfilling life at home, (remember there were six young McConochies!), and his career at sea. He obviously read the works of many poets, and I think his style was mostly influenced by that of Samuel Taylor Coleridge. I, too, have been influenced by him in using 'poetic licence' in the title of this book, 'Rhymes from an Ancient Mariner'.

I hope you have enjoyed them as much as I have.

Norman H McConochie
January 2012